Community
BUILDERS

Brigham Young

Community BUILDERS

Brigham Young

Mormon and Pioneer

by Charnan Simon

Children's Press®
A Division of Grolier Publishing
New York London Hong Kong Sydney
Danbury, Connecticut

Photo Credits

Photographs ©: Archive Photos: 7 (American Stock), 3 (Earl Young), 15; Corbis-Bettmann: cover, 8, 13, 38; Courtesy Museum of Art, Brigham Young University. All Rights reserved.: 31, 35 (C.C.A. Christensen); Daughters of the Utah Pioneers, Salt Lake City, Utah: 27; Folio, Inc.: 2 (Rene Sheret), 45 (Jeff Stapleton/MR); Frank Jensen: 39; Tom Kazunas: 48; LDS Historic Department Archives: 18, 23, 28, 34, 41; Mark Philbrich: 24; Mr.& Mrs. William E. Hill: 30; North Wind Picture Archives: 17, 22; Oregon Historical Society: 33 (#OrHi13137); Salt Lake Convention & Visitor's Bureau: 44; Steve Greenwood: back cover; Utah State Historical Society: 14, 21, 43; Western Heritage Photo Collection: 36 (painting by George Simon).
Map (pp. 10-11) by XNR Productions.

Reading Consultant
Linda Cornwell, Learning Resource Consultant
Indiana Department of Education

Visit Children's Press on the Internet at:
http://publishing.grolier.com

Library of Congress Cataloging-in-Publication Data

Simon, Charnan.
    Brigham Young : Mormon and pioneer / by Charnan Simon.
        p. cm. — (Community builders)
    Includes bibliographical references and index.
    Summary: Presents a biography of the religious leader, from his childhood in Vermont to his rise as the leader of the Mormon Church.
    ISBN: 0-516-20392-4 (lib. bdg.)   0-516-26344-7 (pbk.)
    1. Young, Brigham, 1801-1877—Juvenile literature. 2. Church of Jesus Christ of Latter-Day Saints—Presidents—Biography—Juvenile literature. 3. Mormon Church—Presidents—Biography—Juvenile literature. [1. Young, Brigham, 1801-1877. 2. Church of Jesus Christ of Latter-Day Saints—Presidents. 3. Mormon Church—Presidents.] I. Title. II. Series.
BX8695.Y7S45   1998
289.3'092—dc21
[B]   97-45696
                                                                                                CIP
                                                                                                 AC

Contents

The Mormon Trail

Do you like reading stories about pioneers? In some ways, the story of the United States is the story of pioneers. From its beginning, our country has been settled by pioneers who were looking for a better life.

Brigham Young was one such pioneer. One hundred and fifty years ago, Young was the leader of The Church of Jesus Christ of Latter-day Saints. Members of this church are often called "Mormons,"

Pioneer families loaded their belongings in covered wagons
and headed west in groups called wagon trains.

Brigham Young

for their belief in The Book of Mormon, or "Latter-day Saints." The church was started in 1830. From the beginning, Mormons had trouble finding a place where they could practice their religion in peace. They were driven out of communities in Ohio, Missouri, and Illinois. Their neighbors didn't like the way Mormons lived and worshipped.

Finally, Brigham Young decided it was time for the

Westward Movement

The history of the United States is a history of westward movement. Colonists from Europe began to settle along the Atlantic coast of North America in the early 1600s. Some of them came looking for land. Others were seeking religious freedom.

By the 1700s, pioneers had moved west into the Appalachian Mountains, and then into Pennsylvania and the Ohio River Valley. By the early 1800s, settlers had reached the Mississippi River. By the middle of the 1800s, pioneers were looking beyond the Rocky Mountains to the lands of the far west. By 1860, more than 300,000 settlers had arrived in the West.

Mormons to move west. Between 1847 and 1868, he helped nearly seventy thousand Mormons move to new homes in what later became Salt Lake City, Utah, and other areas of the West. The route the Mormons followed became known as the Mormon Trail.

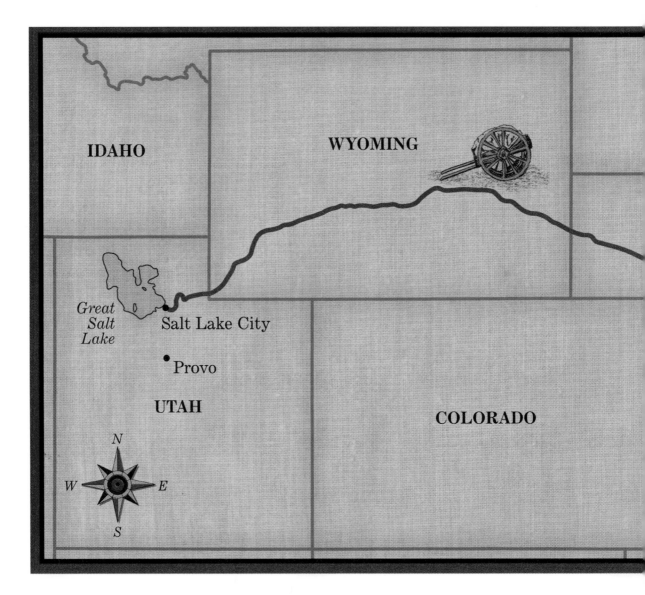

In Utah Territory, Brigham Young found the freedom he was seeking. The Mormon community in Salt Lake City thrived, and Young became the first governor of the territory. He continued to lead the Latter-day Saints until he died in 1877.

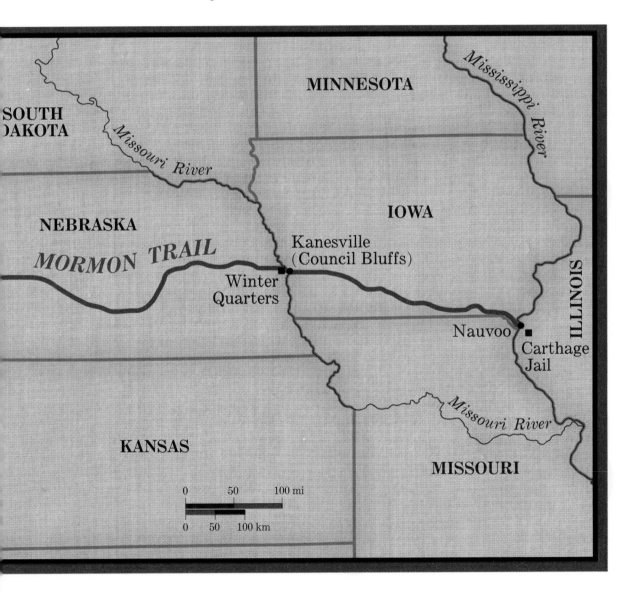

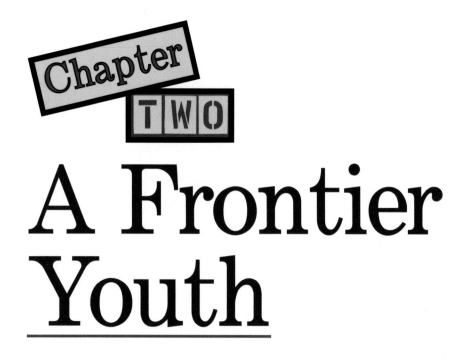

Chapter TWO

A Frontier Youth

Brigham Young was born on June 1, 1801, in the tiny frontier community of Whitingham, Vermont. Frontier life was hard for the Young family. Brigham's father, John, worked hard to make a living on his rocky Vermont farm, and later, in New York. His mother, Nabby, cared for baby Brigham and his eight older brothers and sisters. The children all helped, too. Frontier families had to work together to survive.

Brigham's mother died when he was fourteen years old. By the time Brigham was sixteen, he had left home. He was determined to make his own way

Frontier families lived far from settled areas, and survival was difficult.

in life—but not by farming. For the next ten years, Brigham did many jobs. He painted houses, built cabinets, and repaired furniture. He worked in a pail factory, a shipyard, and a tannery (a place where animal hides are turned into leather). Wherever he went, Brigham earned a reputation for being a hard worker.

In 1824, Brigham married a young woman named Miriam Works. Their first daughter, Elizabeth, was born in 1825. A second daughter, Vilate, followed in 1830. Brigham set up his own furniture-making business. The future looked bright.

Miriam Works

Then Miriam got sick. She was too ill to care for Elizabeth and Vilate or to do household chores. Brigham had to shut down his furniture shop to take care of his family.

Brigham's religious beliefs helped him through this hard time. He had been a Methodist since he was a child. Now he became interested in the teachings of a man named Joseph Smith. Smith was starting a new religion called The Church of Jesus Christ of Latter-day Saints, whose followers were often called "Mormons." For two years, Brigham learned all he could about this religion.

Finally, on April 14, 1832, Brigham Young decided to become a Mormon. It was a decision that would change his life.

Joseph Smith

Joseph Smith (1805–44) was the founder of The Church of Jesus Christ of Latter-day Saints. As a youth, Joseph Smith claimed to have spoken to God. He said that an angel named Moroni had shown him a set of gold plates. These plates were engraved with the history of an ancient American civilization. Smith published this story as the Book of Mormon in 1830. Then, using the Bible and the Book of Mormon as his holy scriptures,

Smith founded his new church on April 6, 1830. Today, there are more than ten million Mormons throughout the world. The church headquarters is located in Salt Lake City, Utah.

Joseph Smith founded
The Church of Jesus Christ
of Latter-day Saints in 1830.

The Young Saint

Brigham Young joined The Church of Jesus Christ of Latter-day Saints for many reasons. He liked the way the temple was the center of Mormon life. He liked the way Mormons worked together, like one big family. Perhaps most important, Brigham believed that Joseph Smith was a prophet of God.

Brigham Young became a lay priest in the church. This meant that even though he was not an official priest, he could preach sermons, baptize new members, and help set up new congregations. Young

Brigham Young's powerful preaching brought many
new followers to the church.

The Kirtland Temple, in Ohio, about 1860

had always been a hard worker. Now that he had something he truly believed in, there was no stopping him. Soon Brigham was traveling all over New England, spreading Joseph Smith's teachings.

The fall of 1832 brought both sad times and joyous ones to Brigham Young. On September 8, his wife Miriam died. Young was heartbroken, but convinced that he would see Miriam again in Heaven. He left his two daughters with family friends and continued his church work. The joyous time came in October, when Young met Joseph Smith for the first time. Brigham Young said, "My joy was full at the privilege of shaking the hand of the prophet of God."

For the next several years, Young did all he could for Joseph Smith and the church. He visited Canada to bring in new church members. He moved to Kirtland, Ohio, where Smith lived, and helped build the Kirtland Temple. He traveled to Missouri to help a group of Mormons who were being attacked by their non-Mormon neighbors. In February 1835, Smith rewarded Brigham by making him a member of the Council of Twelve Apostles.

Council of Twelve Apostles

The Mormon Council of Twelve Apostles is modeled on Jesus' twelve apostles in the New Testament of the Bible. The original twelve apostles helped spread Jesus' teachings. Mormon apostles do the same, as they understand the teachings from the Bible and the Book of Mormon. They travel around the world, bringing in new church members. Under the direction of the church president, or prophet, they oversee the church throughout the world.

There was more good news. In Kirtland, Brigham Young met a woman named Mary Ann Angell. They were married in February 1834.

Brigham Young grew busier than ever. He made more long trips throughout the United States and Canada. He preached at the Kirtland Temple he had

Mary Ann Angell

helped build. When Joseph Smith got into money trouble (he started a bank that failed, losing money for many people), Young helped the Kirtland Mormon community move to a place called Far West, Missouri.

Missouri wasn't a good place for Joseph Smith and his followers. Many Missourians disliked the Mormons' religion and their way of life. Mormons kept to themselves. They shopped at Mormon stores. They sent their children to Mormon schools. They always voted the same way in elections. And Mormons were not tolerant of people who didn't share their belief that Joseph Smith was a prophet of God.

On October 27, 1838, the governor of Missouri gave an "Extermination Order." It said: "The

The Latter-day Saints traveled with handcarts that were large enough to carry 500 pounds (227 kilograms) of supplies, but could be pulled by one or two people.

Mormons must be treated as enemies and must be exterminated [killed] or driven from the state."

Joseph Smith knew his people were in danger. He voluntarily went to prison in exchange for their safety. Meanwhile, Brigham Young helped the other Mormons—nearly fifteen thousand in all—move safely to a new home in Illionis.

By May 1839, Joseph Smith had rejoined his followers in their new community along the Mississippi River. The Mormons named their new home "Nauvoo," from the Hebrew word meaning "beautiful place." They hoped they had at last found a permanent home.

Nauvoo, Illinois, with the town's temple on the hill, in 1845

**Today, Brigham Young's restored home
in Nauvoo is open to visitors.**

By September 1839, Brigham Young was on the move again. This time he went to England. For nearly two years, Young preached the church's gospel in towns all over England. He recruited new Latter-day Saints and helped organize new churches.

Brigham Young enjoyed bringing new followers into the Mormon "family." But he missed his own family in Nauvoo. By now, he and Mary Ann had four children of their own, in addition to Elizabeth and Vilate. Young was worried by letters he received from home. Mary Ann and the children were often ill during the harsh Illinois winters. They were desperately poor, as well. Young did his work in England without pay. He was given a place to stay and food to eat, but not much else. Back home in Nauvoo, Mary Ann had to beg the church leaders for food for the children.

By spring 1841, Young was ready to go home to Illinois. His trip to England had been a huge success. He had preached more than four hundred sermons, and recruited nearly eight thousand new church members.

Chapter FOUR

New Challenges

Nauvoo, Illinois, had changed in Brigham Young's absence. The Mormon city was growing fast. It would soon be one of the largest and richest cities in the United States. Along with this growth came problems. Young's non-Mormon neighbors worried that all of Illinois might turn into a Mormon state.

They worried about other things, too. For example, Nauvoo had its own private army called the Nauvoo Legion. Mormons insisted that the legion was there only to protect Mormons. It would

Brigham Young in the military uniform of the Nauvoo Legion

never attack neighboring communities. But non-Mormons still felt threatened. They also felt threatened by the Mormon practice of plural marriage.

Even Brigham Young was shocked and dismayed when he first heard about plural marriages. "It was the first time in my life I had desired the grave," he later confessed. Brigham was happy with Mary Ann.

He didn't want any new wives. But he also didn't want to go against Joseph Smith's teachings. After much soul-searching, Young decided that Joseph Smith's word was law. He married his first new wife in June 1842. By 1844, he had four wives. Eventually, he had twenty-seven wives and fifty-seven children.

Brigham Young and nineteen of his wives
(Mary Ann is pictured top row, third from right)

Plural Marriage

In 1841, Joseph Smith began preaching the gospel of plural marriage. This meant the taking of more than one wife at the same time. Smith had read in the Bible about prophets who had more than one wife. He believed Mormons should do as Biblical people had done. At first, the Mormons kept this practice a secret. Plural marriage was considered immoral in the United States. Eventually, the secret leaked out. Non-Mormons were horrified at the idea of plural marriages. In 1890, the church ended the practice.

Plural marriages were the last straw as far as the Mormons' Illinois neighbors were concerned. Angry mobs attacked Mormon communities. The state government threatened to make Mormons find somewhere else to live.

Joseph Smith tried doing what he had done in Missouri. He turned himself in to prison in exchange for his followers' safety. But on June 27, 1844, a mob broke into the prison and killed him. The Latter-day Saints had lost their prophet. Suddenly, life in Nauvoo looked very dangerous.

It was time for Brigham Young to act. When Joseph Smith died, Young became the leader of the church. Now the citizens of Nauvoo were his responsibility. Like Moses in the Bible's Old Testament, Brigham Young knew he must lead his people to a new home where they would be safe.

Today, Carthage Jail, the site of Joseph Smith's murder, has been restored to appear as it did in 1844.

This painting, completed in the late 1800s by a Latter-day Saint who traveled the Mormon Trail, shows the Mormons leaving Nauvoo and crossing the frozen Mississippi River.

Moses

Moses was a Hebrew in Egypt at a time when all Hebrews were slaves. According to the Bible, God told Moses to lead his people out of slavery and into the promised land of Canaan. The Hebrews' flight from Egypt is known as the Exodus. As the Hebrews (or Israelites, as they are sometimes called) traveled, they worshipped God in a movable building called a Tabernacle.

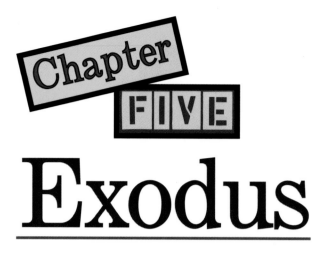

Chapter FIVE

Exodus

In the early 1840s, settlement in the far western United States was just beginning. Fur trappers and mountain men had explored the Rocky Mountains. A few groups of settlers had begun moving into Oregon and California. But there were still huge areas of unsettled land. The Mormons hoped they could finally live in peace if they moved into one of these areas.

The land Brigham Young wanted to settle was called the Great Basin. It was located around the Great Salt Lake in present-day Utah. The Great Basin had good pasture lands and rich soil. It didn't get much rain, but Young was sure an irrigation system could be built to bring water down to the valley

Portland, Oregon, was a young town when this photograph was taken in 1852.

from high mountain streams. Best of all, the Great Basin was a thousand miles from the settled areas of the Midwest. It was also a thousand miles from the settled areas in California and Oregon. There were no neighbors to threaten the Mormons.

Brigham Young quickly organized his followers. The people of Nauvoo, Illinois, began building wagons and gathering supplies. In February 1846, the first Mormons started moving west. The route they

Although this photograph was taken in 1865, these Latter-day Saints and their loaded wagons are similar to the groups who left Nauvoo in 1846.

took exists today and is called the Mormon Trail. Other Mormons soon followed. By September, Nauvoo was almost deserted.

Young had hoped to reach the Great Basin by the end of summer, 1846. But the journey across Iowa was slow and difficult. When the Mormons reached the Missouri River near present-day Omaha, Nebraska, it was almost winter. Young knew it would be unsafe to continue. He decided they should stay where they were until spring.

The Mormons called their new home "Winter Quarters." They built log cabins and dugouts to live in. They set up a brick foundry and wagon-making facilities to help prepare for their journey west.

On April 5, 1847, Brigham Young was ready for the next stage of his journey. Leaving most of the Mormons safe in Winter Quarters, he and a small exploring party set out for the Great Basin. It was a long, hard journey. A typical day started at 5 A.M.

This famous painting shows the Latter-day Saints' Winter Quarters along the Missouri River.

Settlements Along the Mormon Trail

Brigham Young organized the Mormon exodus well. Besides Winter Quarters, Young started other settlements along the Mormon Trail. In each, Mormon pioneers built houses and planted crops. Some settlements ran ferryboats across rivers, and had supply stores. This way, the first Mormon pioneers could help the thousands of others who would follow. These settlements made it much easier and safer for Mormon pioneers to move west.

Kanesville, Iowa, one of the settlements on the Mormon Trail, is known today as Council Bluffs.

with prayers and breakfast. By 7:30 A.M., the company was ready to start out on the trail. A small group of men went first to clear the trail. Next came Brigham Young, at the head of the train of about seventy-two wagons. Armed men rode along the sides and at the end of the wagon train, to guard against danger and to keep the livestock from wandering.

The pioneers ate a quick, cold lunch around noon and were ready to set out again in an hour. By 6:30 P.M., they might have covered 10 miles (16 kilometers). By then, it was time to stop for the night. When the pioneers could find wood, they made campfires and cooked a hot dinner. If there was no wood, they burned dried buffalo droppings, called buffalo chips. Evening prayers came at 8:30 P.M., and bedtime was at 9 P.M.

Brigham Young encouraged the pioneers on the wagon train to share their food and their skills. Blacksmiths and carpenters repaired wagons. Sharpshooters hunted for animals. Women cooked, mended clothing, and cared for the sick. Young knew how important it was for the pioneers to work

In this 1880 photograph, a pioneer woman gathers buffalo chips which, when burned, provided heat and a smokeless fire for cooking.

together. Traveling by wagon train was difficult and dangerous. The Mormons had to cooperate with each other—or risk death.

Finally, all their hard work was rewarded. On July 24, 1847, the wagon train arrived at the Great Basin. In fifteen weeks, the pioneers had traveled nearly 1,300 miles (2,100 km) from Nauvoo. When Brigham Young looked down upon the Great Basin for the first time, he is reported to have said, "It is enough. This is the right place."

Brigham Young didn't waste any time. As soon as he arrived in the valley, he and his followers began

When Brigham Young saw the Great Basin, with Great Salt Lake (right), he knew he and his followers had found the right place to settle.

building homes and planting crops. By fall, Salt Lake City was well under way. Young then returned to Winter Quarters to get the next group of settlers.

The exodus to Salt Lake City continued for the next twenty years. Riding in covered wagons and pushing handcarts, Latter-day Saints from all over the world traveled the Mormon Trail. By 1868, about seventy thousand followers had moved into Salt Lake City and other Mormon communities in the West.

Salt Lake City, Utah

Today, Salt Lake City is the capital and largest city in Utah. It is located about 15 miles (24 km) southeast of the Great Salt Lake. Salt Lake City was founded by Brigham Young on July 24, 1847. It is the world headquarters of The Church of Jesus Christ of Latter-day Saints. More than half of the city's 160,000 residents belong to the church. Salt Lake City is a major center for business, transportation, and the arts.

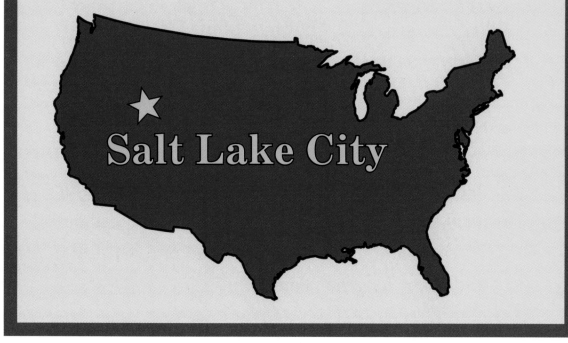

This is an early photograph of Salt Lake City, taken about 1867. The road on the left is East Temple Street, today known as Main Street. Construction on the temple (the large white building near the center) is not yet finished.

Under Brigham Young's leadership, Salt Lake City grew and prospered. Young encouraged his followers to be independent and to cooperate with each other. He was also a firm believer in education. Young founded the University of Deseret (now known as the University of Utah) in 1850, and Brigham Young University in nearby Provo, Utah, in 1875.

Lover of Theater and Music

Brigham Young was a strong supporter of music and the arts. He built the Salt Lake Theatre in 1860. He also made sure that the Mormon Tabernacle included a fine pipe organ. Today, the huge, 11,000-pipe organ accompanies a 325-member choir. This Mormon Tabernacle Choir is world famous for its concerts and recordings.

Brigham Young continued to lead his people until he died in 1877 at the age of seventy-six. Perhaps more than any other person, he helped to shape The Church of Jesus Christ of Latter-day Saints. He is also considered one of the greatest colonizers in U.S. history for his success in bringing thousands of settlers over the Mormon Trail. Brigham Young may have described himself best when he said, "When I think of myself, I think just this—I have the grit in me, and I will do my duty anyhow."

Brigham Young in 1876, shortly before his death

In Your Community

Brigham Young first saw the place that would become Salt Lake City on July 24, 1847. July 24 is celebrated as Pioneer Day by Mormons and is a state holiday in Utah. Do you know when your community was founded? Does your town have a

Timeline

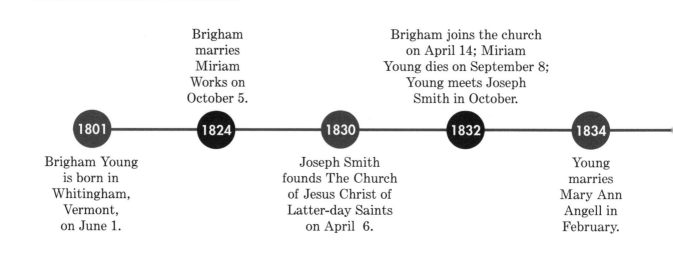

Brigham marries Miriam Works on October 5.

Brigham joins the church on April 14; Miriam Young dies on September 8; Young meets Joseph Smith in October.

| 1801 | 1824 | 1830 | 1832 | 1834 |

Brigham Young is born in Whitingham, Vermont, on June 1.

Joseph Smith founds The Church of Jesus Christ of Latter-day Saints on April 6.

Young marries Mary Ann Angell in February.

Founders' Day parade or picnic? Find out about how and when your community began, and learn what you can do to help celebrate this important date.

While you are learning about your community's history, find out who the earliest settlers were. Does your community have a large population of any one ethnic group or nationality? How long has your family lived in the area? Where were you and your parents and your grandparents born? Ask an adult to help you trace your own family history!

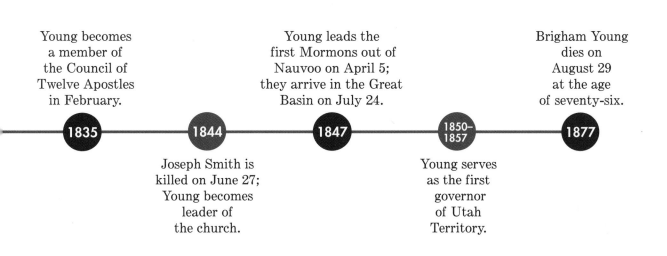

Young becomes a member of the Council of Twelve Apostles in February.

1835

Joseph Smith is killed on June 27; Young becomes leader of the church.

1844

Young leads the first Mormons out of Nauvoo on April 5; they arrive in the Great Basin on July 24.

1847

Young serves as the first governor of Utah Territory.

1850–1857

Brigham Young dies on August 29 at the age of seventy-six.

1877

To Find Out More

Here are some additional resources to help you learn more about Brigham Young, The Church of Jesus Christ of Latter-day Saints, and the Mormon Trail:

Books

Fradin, Dennis Brindell. *Utah.* Children's Press, 1993.

Green, Carl R. and Sanford, William R. *Brigham Young, Pioneer and Mormon Leader.* Enslow Publishers, Inc., 1996.

Hill, William E. *Finding the Right Place: The Story of the Mormon Trail.* Oregon-California Trails Association, 1996.

Levine, Ellen. *If You Traveled West in a Covered Wagon.* Scholastic, Inc., 1986.

Wyss, Thelma H. *Show Me Your Rocky Mountains.* Deseret Book Co., 1989.

Organizations and Online Sites

The Church of Jesus Christ of Latter-day Saints
Public Affairs Dept.
15 E. South Temple
Salt Lake City, UT 84150
http://www.LDS.org

Latter-day Saints Family History Library
35 NW Temple
Salt Lake City, UT 84150

Nauvoo Visitor's Center
P.O. Box 215
Nauvoo, IL 62354

Mormon Visitor's Center
937 W. Walnut
Independence, MO 64050

Mormon Trail Center
3215 State St.
Omaha, NE 68112

This Is the Place State Park
2601 Sunnyside Ave.
Salt Lake City, UT 84107

Index

About the Author

Charnan Simon lives in Madison, Wisconsin, with her husband, Tom Kazunas, and her daughters Ariel and Hana. Charnan is a former editor of *Cricket Magazine* and sometimes works at a children's bookstore called Pooh Corner. Mainly, however, she likes reading and writing books and spending time with her family.

Charnan still remembers the first time she visited Salt Lake City. She drove into the city at night, and when she woke up the next morning she was astonished at how beautiful the valley was—and how majestically the Wasatch Mountains loomed over it. It is no wonder Brigham Young said, "This is the place."

My dear Rose,

Now that I am leaving the Planet of the Gargand, I can take time to write to you about the adventures Fox and I had here.

It's a marvelous planet with wishing-trees whose roots hold the planet together. Every so often, all the trees disappear at the same time, and the seeds of new trees must be sown before the planet breaks apart. Many people strive for the honor of being the Gargand, the one who plants these seeds. It is a dangerous mission, but the future of the whole planet is at risk.

On the Planet of the Gargand, I was glad to meet exceptional people who were willing to risk their own safety to help others. These people give me the courage and hope that one day the Snake may no longer endanger anyone's planet.

The Little Prince

First American edition published in 2014 by Graphic Universe™.

Le Petit Prince ™

based on the masterpiece by Antoine de Saint-Exupéry

© 2014 LPPM
An animated series based on the novel *Le Petit Prince* by Antoine de Saint-Exupéry
Developed for television by Matthieu Delaporte, Alexandre de la Patellière, and Bertrand Gatignol
Directed by Pierre-Alain Chartier

© 2014 ÉDITIONS GLÉNAT
Copyright © 2014 by Lerner Publishing Group, Inc., for the current edition

Graphic Universe™
A division of Lerner Publishing Group, Inc.
241 First Avenue North
Minneapolis, MN 55401 U.S.A.

For reading levels and more information, look up this title at www.lernerbooks.com.

Library of Congress Cataloging-in-Publication Data

Bruneau, Clotilde.
    [Planète de Géhom. English]
    The planet of Gehom / story by Thierry Gaudin ; design and illustrations by Elyum Studio ; adaptation by Clotilde Bruneau ; translation, Anne Collins Smith and Owen Smith. — 1st American edition.
        p.   cm. — (The little prince ; #16)
    ISBN 978-0-7613-8766-4 (lib. bdg. : alk. paper)
    ISBN 978-1-4677-2426-5 (eBook)
    1. Graphic novels. I. Gaudin, Thierry. II. Smith, Anne Collins, translator. III. Smith, Owen (Owen M.), translator. IV. Saint-Exupéry, Antoine de, 1900-1944. Petit Prince. V. Elyum Studio. VI. Petit Prince (Television program) VII. Title.
    PZ7.7.B8Ph 2014
    741.5`944—dc23   2013028757

Manufactured in the United States of America
1 — PC — 12/31/13.

THE NEW ADVENTURES
BASED ON THE MASTERPIECE BY ANTOINE DE SAINT-EXUPÉRY

The Little Prince

THE PLANET OF GEHOM

Based on the animated series and an original story by Thierry Gaudin

Design: Elyum Studio
Story: Clotilde Bruneau
Artistic Direction: Didier Poli
Art: Audrey Bussi
Backgrounds: Isa Python
Coloring: Karine Lambin
Editing: Christine Chatal
Editorial Consultant: Didier Convard

Translation: Anne and Owen Smith

Graphic Universe™ • Minneapolis

★ THE LITTLE PRINCE

The Little Prince has extraordinary gifts. His sense of wonder allows him to discover what no one else can see. The Little Prince can communicate with all the beings in the universe, even the animals and plants. His powers grow over the course of his adventures.

The Prince's uniform:
When he transforms into the uniform of a prince, he is more agile and quick. When faced with difficult situations, the Little Prince also uses a sword that lets him sketch and bring to life anything from his imagination.

His sketchbook:
When he is not in his Prince's clothing, the Little Prince carries a sketchbook. When he blows on the pages, they take wing and form objects that he'll find very useful. Like his sword, it's powered by stardust collected on his travels.

★ FOX

A grouch, a trickster, and, so he says, interested only in his next meal, Fox is in reality the Little Prince's best friend. As such, he is always there to give him help but also just as much to help him to grow and to learn about the world.

★ THE SNAKE

Even though the Little Prince still does not know exactly why, there can be no doubt that the Snake has set his mind to plunging the entire universe into darkness! And to accomplish his goal, this malicious being is ready to use any form of deception. However, the Snake never takes action himself. He prefers to bring out the wickedness in those beings he has chosen to bite, tempting them to put their own worlds in danger.

★ THE GLOOMIES

When people who have been "bitten" by the Snake have completely destroyed their own planets, they become Gloomies, slaves to their Snake master. The Gloomies act as a group and carry out the Snake's most vile orders so he can get the better of the Little Prince!

4

CUBIONS! PREPARE FOR THE GREAT PIVOT!

WHEW-- IT'S OVER! WE CAN REST AWHILE.

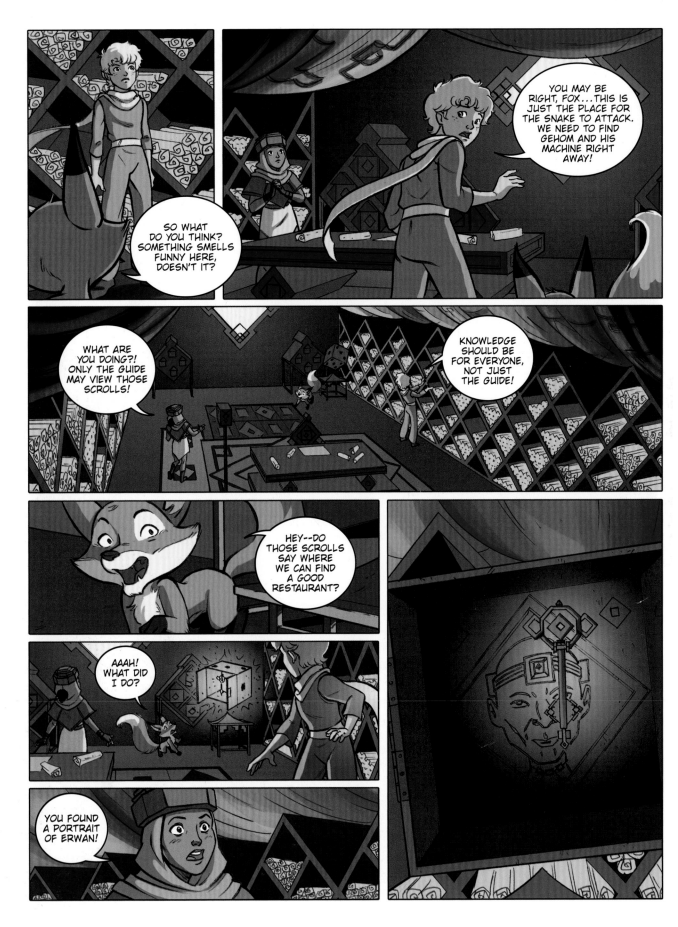

19

24

31

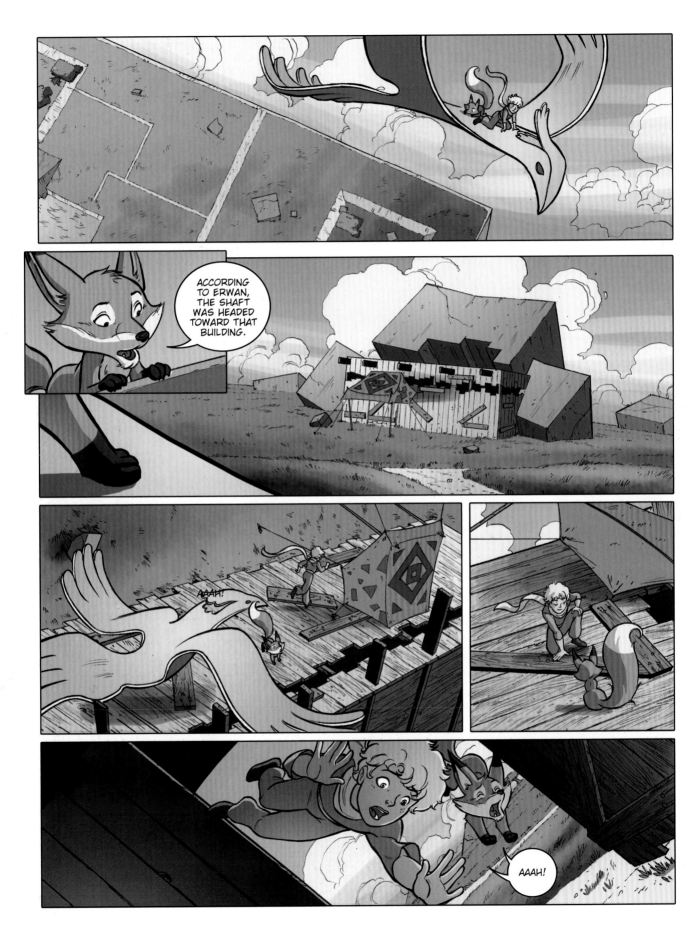

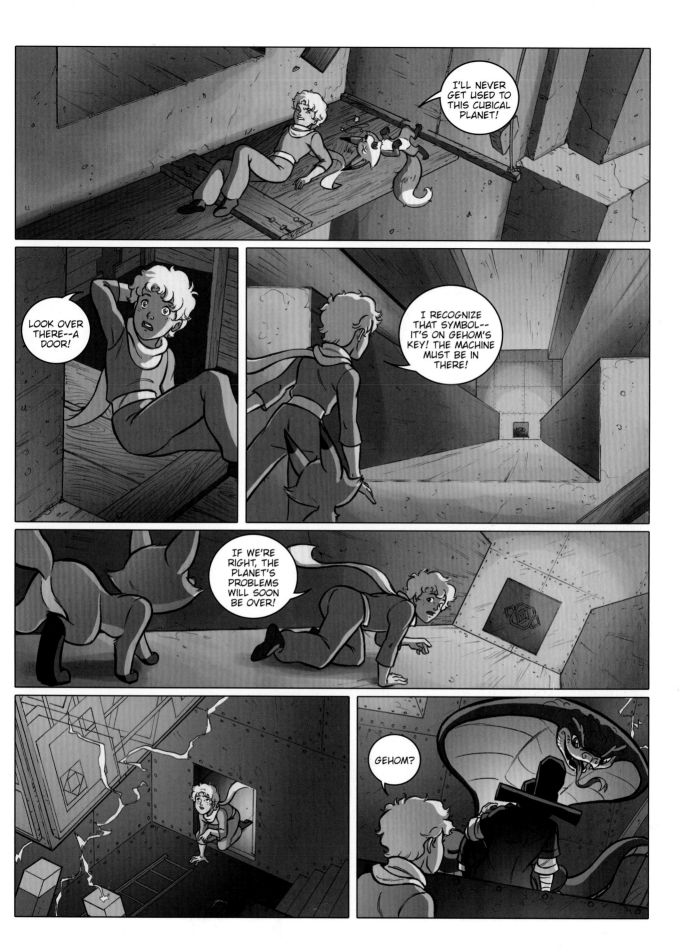

35

I'VE BROUGHT YOUR KEY--NOW YOU CAN FREE YOUR PEOPLE FROM THE MACHINE!

NO MATTER-- I'VE SPRUNG MY TRAP!

YOU FOUND IT!

WHETHER YOU LET THE MACHINE RUN OR STOP IT WITH YOUR KEY, THE CUBIONS ARE DOOMED!

THE GLOOMIES MUST BE BLOCKING THE ROAD! IF THE PLANET PIVOTS, EVERYONE WILL BE FLUNG INTO SPACE!

BUT IF WE DON'T LET IT PIVOT, THEY'LL DIE OF THIRST IN A DESERT!

HOW WILL GEHOM KNOW WHEN TO STOP THE MACHINE?

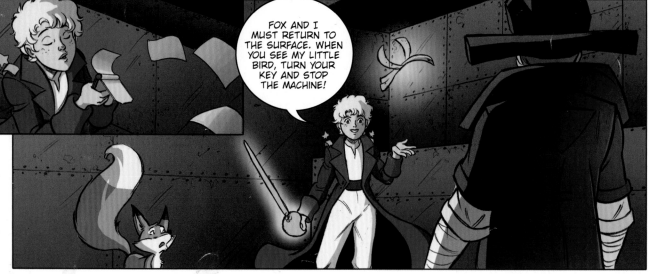

FOX AND I MUST RETURN TO THE SURFACE. WHEN YOU SEE MY LITTLE BIRD, TURN YOUR KEY AND STOP THE MACHINE!

AAARGH! WE CAN'T BREAK THROUGH!

IT'S TIME FOR YOU TO MAKE A CHOICE! EITHER WAIT HERE FOR THE GREAT PIVOT AND BE FLUNG INTO SPACE...

...OR KNEEL BEFORE ME AND OBEY MY COMMANDS!

HURRY! THE GREAT PIVOT IS ABOUT TO START!

DO WE HAVE TIME TO REPLACE THE OLD SQUARE WHEELS ON THE CASTLE?

YES! IF EVERYONE HELPS, WE CAN STILL MAKE IT!

43

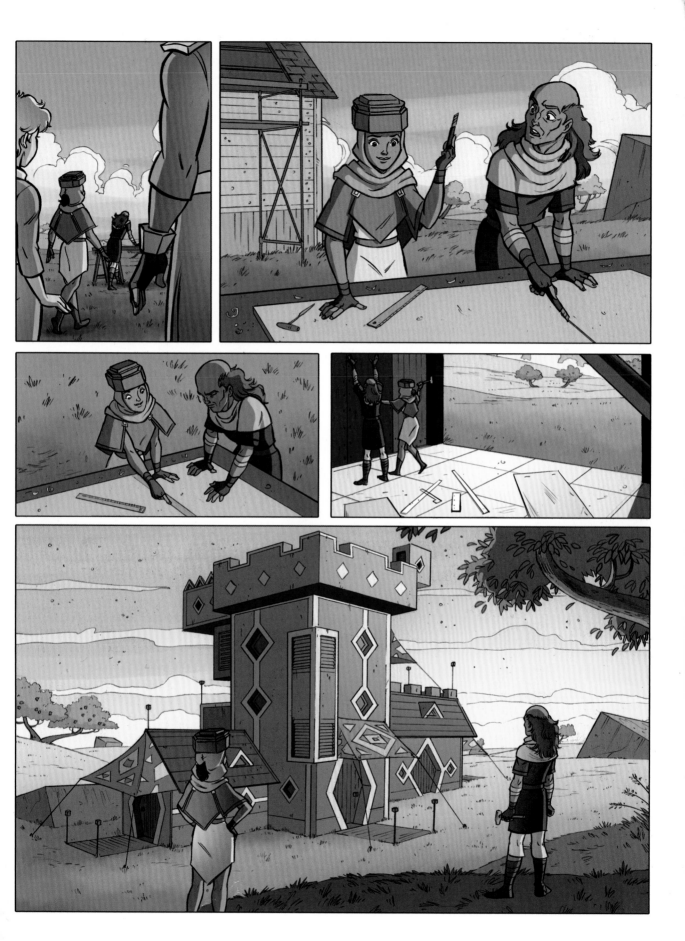